The University of Georgia
Trivia Book

The University of Georgia
TRIVIA BOOK

F.N. Boney

Hill Street Press  Athens, Georgia

A HILL STREET PRESS BOOK

Published in the United States of America by
Hill Street Press LLC
191 East Broad Street, Suite 209 • Athens, Georgia 30601-2848 USA
706-613-7200
info@hillstreetpress.com • www.hillstreetpress.com

Hill Street Press is committed to preserving the written word. Every effort is made to print books on acid-free paper with a significant amount of post-consumer recycled content. • Hill Street Press books are available in bulk purchase and customized editions to institutions and corporate accounts. Please contact us for more information. • No material in this book may be reproduced, scanned, stored, or transmitted in any form, including all electronic and print media, or otherwise used without the prior written consent of the publisher. However, an excerpt not to exceed ten entries may be used one time only by newspaper and magazine editors solely in conjunction with a review of or feature article about this book, the author, or Hill Street Press, LLC. Attribution must be provided including the publisher's name, author's name, and title of the book.

Copyright © 2004 by Hill Street Press. All rights reserved.
Text and cover design by Anne Richmond Boston.
Printed in the United States of America.

Library of Congress Cataloging-in-Publication Data

Boney, F. N.
    The University of Georgia trivia book / by F.N. Boney.
      p.   cm.
    ISBN 1-58818-088-3 (alk. paper)
    1. University of Georgia—Miscellanea. I. Title.
  LD1981.8 .B66 2002
  378.758'18—dc21   2002006070

ISBN # 1-58818-088-3
10 9 8 7 6 5 4 3 2 1

First Printing

Contents

Preface vii

Introduction ix

Students 1

Faculty 23

Alumni 37

Leaders 55

Town-gown 65

Government 81

Buildings and Grounds 91

Sports 115

Further Reading 143

Preface

This volume is derived from over two decades of researching and publishing at the University of Georgia. To thank everyone who contributed over this long haul would be impractical, but recognition of those who helped me significantly with this specific project is needed. Many thanks to Steven Brown and Gilbert Head and their fellows in the Hargrett Library, Tom Jackson and Larry Dendy and their troops in Public Affairs, Claude Felton and his gang in Sports Information, Fran Lane and her tour guides at the Visitors Center, former Associate Vice President Tom Bowen, University Professor of Higher Education Tom Dyer, and, of course, indirectly, two centuries worth of faculty and staff and students who are the main subject of this study.

This little volume contains about 500 questions and answers covering more than two centuries of UGA's development. Organized chronologically under headings such as "students" and "alumni" and "sports," it presents the trivial and the bizarre, the interesting and the significant, all mixed together and often overlapping. In this unique fashion it tells the story of one American university—and in a broad way all of them. My old schools, Hampden-Sydney College and the University of Virginia, and even Georgia's fiercest rivals, the Georgia Techs and Auburns and Floridas, have similar stories to tell, full of irony and humor, frustration and success, but ultimately All-American in their relentless (and realistic) optimism.

So relax and enjoy this new presentation of the adventures of a Southern and American school, unique and also typical. UGA is headed along a bumpy road that goes onward and upward. Come along for the ride!

Introduction

The University of Georgia is an old school, and by American standards very old. Chartered as the first state university by the Georgia legislature in 1785, UGA began classes in 1801 as the new town of Athens began growing around it.

Progress was slow in a state that was largely rural and often frontier. By 1861, when the Civil War erupted, UGA had only about one hundred students, and as late as 1900, only about three hundred. In reality, UGA operated as an all white, all male, church-related, private liberal arts college that served an infinitesimally small percentage of the state's population.

Some change did occur in the last decades of the nineteenth century, especially after UGA became a federal land-grant college in 1872. The rigid old curriculum diversified a little, and the rigid old discipline relaxed some too. Social fraternities emerged, and intercollegiate athletics, especially football, arrived in 1892. A few new buildings sprang up. The faculty grew slowly along with the student body, and a few even had the specialized new Ph.D. degree.

Dramatic change came with Chancellor Walter B. Hill in 1899 as the state's population passed 2,200,000. A real state university began to emerge, slowly at first, but more and more rapidly as the twentieth century matured. In 1918 white women were finally admitted as undergraduates, and enrollment passed one thousand for the first time. A booming agricultural program spearheaded the new south campus that gradually emerged as a citadel of science and technology. Hard times in the 1920s and 1930s did not keep enrollment from climbing into the three thousands.

The whole nation surged forward during World War II, and the state of Georgia never stopped to look back. At last a dynamic economy poured money into UGA, and it prospered greatly. As enrollment approached nine thousand in 1961, the admission of the first two African American undergraduates removed the last barrier from the past, and since then UGA has flourished as never before. Enrollment has zoomed to over thirty-two thousand, the campus has sprawled out in all directions, and new buildings have grown larger and higher as available space becomes scarce within the town-turned-city of Athens.

Quality has advanced even faster than quantity as the old school gains increasing national and international recognition. Finally, UGA stands tall, reflecting the dreams and efforts of generations of professors and students and staff—and indeed generations of the people of Georgia. And remember, as the questions and answers unfold, the best is yet to come!

> "To form the youth, the rising hope of our land."
> —**Charter 1785**

Students

What does the original charter mean by "the rising hope of our land"?

The younger generations ("the youth")

When did classes actually start?

1801

According to the University's rules of 1803, what was the penalty for blasphemy, robbery, fornication, or theft?

Expulsion

Which two foreign languages were stressed in the early classical education?

Greek and Latin

During the administration of Presbyterian President Moses Waddel, 1819–1829, how often was chapel attendance required?

Twice a day and only regular church on Sunday

> "Nearly extinct, consisting of only seven students with three professors"
> —President Moses Waddel on UGA in 1819

Who was the unruly student President Waddel expelled ("sent away") in 1828 who later became a leading politician and Confederate general?

Robert Toombs

The historical marker by the Chapel depicts the legendary (almost surely untrue) exploits of what early student?

Robert Toombs

What were the two literary societies that competed passionately against one another?

Demosthenian (1803) and Phi Kappa (1820)

This early rivalry was especially intense in what activity?

Enrolling prominent people as honorary members

Who were a few "big fish" netted by the literary societies before the Civil War?

Phi Kappas: Andrew Jackson, James K. Polk, Jefferson Davis

Demosthenians: William Gilmore Simms, Henry Clay, Andrew Johnson

What were the main offenses that early students were disciplined for?

Disorderly conduct and drunkenness

What small, sickly student, one of the few on scholarship, compiled an outstanding record before graduating in 1832 and became a famous politician and vice president of the Confederacy?

Alexander H. Stephens

> "Breakfast: coffee and tea, corn and wheat bread, butter, bacon or beef."
> —UGA menu before Civil War

"On to Watkinsville"
—1898 *Pandora*

Who was the first foreign student?

John D. Diomatari (a Greek)

What two students who later became famous shared a dormitory room in Old College in 1832?

Alexander H. Stephens and Crawford W. Long

Who graduated in 1832, studied medicine at the University of Pennsylvania, and in the 1840s in the Athens area performed some of the first operations using ether as an anesthetic?

Crawford W. Long

What was his nickname at Georgia?

"Baby" (because he was younger than his classmates)

What student wrote an interesting unpublished diary of daily life on the campus in the early 1840s?

Charles Barrington King (on microfilm at the State Archives in Atlanta)

> "Who, on each side fought for the thing they loved."
> —Poem on Civil War soldiers delivered at UGA on 6 May 1933 by **Stephen Vincent Benet**

Student Edward Spann Hammond described what dramatic event in his 1852 diary?

A fight between two students in which one almost died after being stabbed with a sword cane

What was the financial status of most families who sent their sons to UGA before the Civil War?

Well-to-do but not rich

What were the main food staples in the antebellum dining halls?

Pork, poultry, and corn

What was a recurring problem in the dining halls throughout the nineteenth century?

Food fights

> "Most of the streakers were probably liberal arts majors."
> —*Atlanta Journal*
> 26 April 1989

According to the catalogue of 1856–1857, what was the annual cost of tuition, room rent, library fee, and servant's hire?

$50 (with another $114 for meals)

What was the first campus publication, founded in 1851 and appearing off and on through the 1890s?

The Georgia University Magazine

Before the Civil War what provision was made for students not quite ready for regular college courses?

The Grammar School on campus and later the University High School in North Athens

During the Civil War what finally carried away most of the dwindling student population and caused UGA to close by the summer of 1864?

The Confederate draft, instituted in 1862 and steadily expanded as losses soared

What was the high point of the civil engineering program instituted after the Civil War?

A week-long field trip in the spring in which students camped out and surveyed a railroad line

When did wounded or indigent war veterans first receive benefits at UGA?

Immediately after the Civil War

Defying Reconstruction edicts, what rebel veteran and member of the class of 1868 posed for a class photograph in 1866 still wearing his Confederate uniform?

George Dalton Bancroft (top graduate of the class of 1868)

> "To function in almost any occupation, our students must have an international perspective."
> —**Han Park**

What junior undergraduate delivered a speech at the 1867 commencement that criticized Reconstruction and hailed the Lost Cause—and almost got UGA closed down by Union General John Pope in Atlanta?

Albert H. Cox (later a prominent lawyer)

What youngster in the class of 1868, about the only non-veteran, whose father had been killed in action at Petersburg in 1864, later became the famous editor of the *Atlanta Constitution*?

Henry W. Grady

In 1866, what was the first Greek-letter fraternity to appear on campus?

Sigma Alpha Epsilon

What student was expelled for a year for fighting but returned to graduate in 1874 and became an outstanding faculty member, dean, and finally chancellor from 1906 to 1925?

David C. "Uncle Dave" Barrow

What was the main objective of the Irish Club in 1896?

Just having fun

What was the name of Georgia's yearbook, one of the first in the South in 1886, and who published it for many years?

The *Pandora*, the fraternities

What two students at the end of the nineteenth century left excellent photographs of campus life at that time?

Telamon Cuyler (B.L., 1893) and William Munroe White (B.S., 1900)

"In June 1920, eleven women received undergraduate degrees, the first ever given for work in residence."

—*Pandora* **1928**

What were the first drama clubs in the 1890s?

The Thalians and the Blackfriars

Founded in 1893 and independent since 1980, what is the name of the student newspaper?

The Red and Black

When did Phi Beta Kappa award UGA a chapter?

1914

What shocking event occurred around 2 A.M. on January 30, 1918, when two non-students, a boy, twenty, and a girl, seventeen, from Jefferson, visited friends in their dormitory room?

A murder-suicide

When were white women admitted as undergraduates?

1918

> "If any scholar shall assault, strike, or wound the President, a Professor, or a Tutor or shall designedly break their doors or windows, he shall be expelled."
>
> **—University of Georgia Code of Laws, 1803**

When did UGA's enrollment first top one thousand?

1919 (following the admission of women)

When did neighboring universities admit undergraduate women?

The University of Alabama 1892, the University of Tennessee 1893, the University of South Carolina 1895 (and the University of Virginia 1968!)

How many women received undergraduate degrees in June 1920?

Eleven

After women were admitted in 1918 what was one of the first clubs they organized?

The rifle team

> "... spoke to [Robert] Toombs about swearing."
> —President Moses Waddel

Before women were admitted what did librarian Duncan Burnet sometimes complain of?

"Trifling loungers"

After the admission of women what was the new complaint?

"Would be lovers" who came to the library to "jelly"

According to the *Pandora* of 1923, what percentage of students were church members and what percentage attended church?

82%, 86%

What was the name of the formal spring dance in the early twentieth century?

Little Commencement

In 1921, what was the first sorority on campus?

Phi Mu

Who were the first two women to graduate from the law school in 1825?

Gussie Brooks and Edith Elizabeth House

What women's group, organized in 1927, presented an annual water pageant in the pool in the Women's Physical Education Building?

The Dolphin Club

What was the name of the alternative newspaper published on campus only once on March 14, 1927, before its five editors were expelled (and soon reinstated)?

The Iconoclast

In the 1930s what was the "monkey drill" performed by the R.O.T.C calvarymen?

Horseback acrobatics

Students **13**

In a dramatic coup in 1937 who did the Phi Kappa Literary Society initiate as an honorary member and where?

President Franklin D. Roosevelt at Warm Springs, Georgia

What leader of this coup won a Rhodes Scholarship, successfully challenged the state's county-unit voting system before the Supreme Court in 1963, and later defended Martin Luther King in court?

Morris B. Abram

The Voluntary Religious Association in the 1930s was the successor of what groups?

The Y.M.C.A. and the Y.W.C.A.

What sorority bought the old "wedding cake" Thomas-Carithers House (1896) on Milledge Avenue in 1939 and thus probably saved it?

Alpha Gamma Delta

In 1944, who was the first female valedictorian?

Eugenie Neel of Atlanta

After World War II how high did enrollment go with the "G.I. Bill" veterans, and what did it drop back down to in the early 1950s after the veterans graduated?

7,800 down to 5,000

Who was the veteran who left UGA before graduating to become a very successful illustrator for *Mad Magazine* and various horror comics?

Jack Davis

Right after World War II what was the very appropriate name of the short-lived, unauthorized student newspaper that featured the cartoons of Jack Davis?

The Bull Sheet

". . . by far the happiest days of my life."

—Alexander H. Stephens, on his time spent at Franklin College

Students

"... to convey stories of knowledge to the student, and abundance of humor and wit to the gay, and gems of poetry to the ladies."

—Aim of the *Georgia University Magazine*, 1855

Which of the two literary societies briefly expired in the early 1950s?

Phi Kappa

When did UGA integrate?

January 1961

Who were the first two African American students?

Charlayne Hunter (now Hunter-Gault) and Hamilton Holmes

What procedure did they use?

They transferred in as juniors from Wayne State University and Morehouse College, respectively

What happened a few days after they began classes?

A riot briefly erupted around Myers Central Dormitory where Hunter lived

Why did Holmes live off campus in Athens while Hunter did not?

> Male students could live off campus, but female students could not

What was one of the last forms of hazing of male freshmen which faded away in the early 1960s?

> The shirt-tail parade in which pantsless (but not underpantsless) males ran around the town and campus

The first significant student protest in the spring of 1968 demanded what?

> Equal rights for women

In the spring of 1970 much larger demonstrations protested what?

> The shooting of students at Kent State University and the Vietnam War

What was the first African American fraternity, organized in 1969?

Alpha Phi Alpha

What was the first African American sorority, organized in 1969?

Delta Sigma Theta

What was destroyed in the 1960s to make way for the extension of the law library?

The Strahan House, one of the three antebellum faculty houses

What old homecoming tradition ended in 1970 as enrollment mushroomed?

The senior parade at Sanford Stadium during halftime of the football game

> "The horticulture garden has helped educate a whole army of dedicated student workers who plant, dig, weed, clean, and worry . . ."
> **—Alan Armitage**

What incident at the 1970 half time contributed to its demise?

Harassment of Mississippi cheerleaders and other "offensive behavior"

What national collegiate craze swept through UGA in the spring of 1974?

Streaking

By 2000, where did most undergraduates come from?

The Atlanta area

Which two Georgia counties now send the most undergraduate students to UGA?

Cobb and Gwinnett Counties (suburban Atlanta)

What are the major achievements of the modern Student Government Association?

Unknown

How many Rhodes Scholars had UGA produced by 2000?

Eighteen

In 2000, what was the percentage of African American undergraduates?

6–7%

In 2000, what percentage of students were from foreign countries?

5%

In 2001, how do the Greeks breakdown?

Four African American fraternities, four African American sororities, twenty-four white fraternities, eighteen white sororities

Where are the most attractive women undergraduates concentrated in the nation?

> The University of Georgia—and all of the other deep Southern universities from Columbia, South Carolina to Austin, Texas

When did women clearly outnumber men on campus as undergraduates?

> During World War II and now

What modern major has had the most dramatic shift from virtually all male to overwhelmingly female?

> Veterinary medicine

Roughly what was the male-female ratio of first-year students at the law school in 2000?

> 50-50

> "Your son is greatly neglecting his College duties."
> —Letter from faculty to parent on 7 March 1860

> "I know there's a big Italian population in the Northeast, but I had no idea there were that many Greeks here."
>
> —Visitor to the University of Georgia campus, upon hearing that 18% of the UGA student population are "Greeks"

Traditionally, what would have been the stereotypes for Georgia Tech and UGA students?

Tech: nerds (or, more poetically, pencil-necked geeks), UGA: rednecks or bumpkins

Now, what are the stereotypes for Georgia Tech and UGA students?

Tech: yuppies, UGA: yuppies

What did Howard Stern tell his TV audience were the requirements for earning a UGA degree?

A coon-skin cap and a bowl of grits

> "The academic faculty consists of twenty-five members."
> —*Handbook of the University of Georgia* **1903**

Faculty

Who was the first and only professor in 1801 when UGA actually began operations?

Josiah Meigs

Who was the first foreign professor in 1806 and what did he teach?

Monsieur Petit de Chairville taught French (briefly)

What role did the antebellum faculty dislike the most?

Campus policeman

> "The faculty of the University is the heart of the institution."
> —**President O.C. Aderhold, 1951**

What wealthy planter from Hancock County endowed a chair of agriculture in 1854 and who first filled the position?

William Terrell and Daniel Lee

What three Athenians established the law school in 1859?

Thomas R.R. Cobb, Joseph Henry Lumpkin, and William Hope Hull

What young physician taught science in 1858 before moving on to become an outstanding medical scientist and a champion of the germ theory of infection?

Joseph Jones

What tutor, who stayed on after graduating in 1855, fought an epic battle with unruly students and later fought with similar bravery as a Johnny Reb?

William D. Wash

> *"El destino* brought me to Georgia."
> —**Judith Ortiz Cofer**

What two brothers from a wealthy slaveholding family graduated from UGA, taught there in the 1850s, served the Confederacy, and finally moved west to play a major role in the founding of the University of California at Berkeley?

John and Joseph LeConte

What professor had a rough time teaching mathematics, resigned in 1853, prospered in the insurance business, and in 1879 made a gift of bonds to UGA that later paid big dividends?

Charles F. McCay

Identify the two Mells at UGA: the father taught there from 1856 to 1888 and was chancellor from 1878 to 1888, and the son led his class of 1861 and was killed in action at the battle of Crampton's Gap in September 1862.

Patrick Hues Mell and Benjamin Mell

What professor introduced intercollegiate athletics, especially football, in 1892?

Charles H. Herty (class of 1886)

What two professors established a "French Connection" that lasted almost seven decades?

Leon Henri Charbonnier taught mathematics and civil engineering from 1861 to 1898 and Joseph Lustrat taught French from 1897 to 1927

What young professor came from Hampden-Sydney College in Virginia in 1889 to teach Latin and Greek for over half a century and also served as dean of the faculty before retiring in 1945?

Willis H. Bocock

Who was appointed the first dean of the Graduate School in 1910?

Willis H. Bocock

Which professor, when applying for a passport, mentioned that he was born in a foreign country?

Willis H. Bocock, born on January 4, 1865 in Virginia, Confederate States of America

Who came in 1907 to upgrade and invigorate a moribund agricultural program?

Andrew M. Soule

Who was the first female member of the UGA staff?

Miss Sarah A. Frierson, librarian from 1888 to 1910

What distinguished scientist (class of 1841) had two different buildings on campus named for him?

Joseph LeConte. Current Meigs Hall bore his name until the 1950s when a newer building now housing the History Department was given his name

> "I feel fortunate to do something that brings others joy— and make a living at it."
> **—Steve Dancz**

Faculty

> "Good teaching has been a hallmark of the University since 1801 when the first classes were taught by Josiah Meigs . . ."
>
> —**Thomas G. Dyer**

In the friction between the new south campus and the traditional north campus what half-playful epithets were sometimes thrown around?

"Cow college" and "old foggies"

What campus marriage in 1914 symbolized the underlying harmony between the new south campus and the old north campus?

Thomas H. McHatton, head of the Horticulture Department, married Marie Lustrat, oldest daughter of the head of the French Department

What else was unusual about this wedding?

The Catholic bishop of Savannah presided in a new chapel in Athens in the heart of the Protestant Bible belt

> "Don't be afraid to fall in love with something and pursue it with intensity."
> —**E. Paul Torrance**

Who was the first female undergraduate to receive a diploma from UGA, and when was she made head of the Division of Home Economics?

Mary E. Creswell, B.S. 1919, head of the Division of Home Economics, 1918 (these dates are correct)

Who was the first professional librarian at UGA who served for most of the first half of the twentieth century?

Duncan Burnet

What professor in the early 1930s shifted from civil engineering to mathematics to avoid being transferred to Georgia Tech?

Charles M. Strahan

> "I learn from them [students] as much as they learn from me."
> —Bertis Downs IV

What professor of agricultural engineering directed the building boom at UGA and other University System schools in the late 1930s?

R.H. Driftmier

As UGA became more oriented toward research what two professors who both arrived in 1919 and both retired in 1958 gained national recognition for publications?

Julian H. Miller (plant pathology) and E. Merton Coulter (history)

What department did Jules Cesar Alciatore, the heir apparent of New Orleans restaurant Antione's, teach in at UGA?

Romance Languages

> "I as a painter will remain a student for my entire life."
> —**Lamar Dodd**

Who were the five veteran professors who retired in 1945, all with at least a half century of service?

Willis H. Bocock (Greek, 54 years), William Davis Hooper (Latin, 53 years), John H.T. McPherson (history, 51 years), John Morris (German, 50 years), and Charles M. Strahan (mathematics, 61 years)

Besides loyalty, these professors symbolized the passing of what else?

The passing of an influential Virginia-Maryland faculty core and the gradual fading of professors who stressed teaching over publishing

Before World War II why did many professors teach until they dropped?

No state retirement system existed before 1945

> "Everyone has a role in the stewardship of the world and its inhabitants."
> —**Steve Stice**

> "The ecosystem is greater than the sum of its parts."
> —Eugene Odum

When was the *Georgia Review* founded at UGA and by whom?

1947 by Professor John Donald Wade

What conservative Southern literary group did he join in the 1930s?

The Nashville Agrarians (while at Vanderbilt)

What North Carolina native taught Georgia and Southern history from 1919 to 1958, published forty books, and edited the *Georgia Historical Quarterly* for fifty years?

E. Merton Coulter

Following in Coulter's footsteps, what native Georgian taught his beloved state's history from 1949 to 1976, and published twelve books and many articles on that subject?

Kenneth Coleman

What retired New York lawyer enrolled at Georgia as a special student, donated a hundred paintings to UGA, and became the first director of the Georgia Museum of Art?

Alfred H. Holbrook

What native of Fairburn, Georgia, studied architecture at Georgia Tech and art in New York City and from 1937 to 1972 led the Art Department while gaining wide recognition for his own paintings?

Lamar Dodd

What other native of Fairburn, Georgia, won similar recognition as head of the Zoology Department and as an expert on malaria and served as dean of the Graduate School after World War II?

George H. Boyd

"Love is the religion and the universe is the book."

—Coleman Barks

> "Do anything you want to a human, but don't kill any animals in my class."
>
> —Harriette Austin, creative writing teacher

When registration was a mass affair with considerable confusion in the Coliseum, who was the "master of ceremonies," easily located wearing his baseball cap?

Dean William Tate

Who was the first African American professor, hired in 1968?

Richard M. Graham, a specialist in music therapy

Who came to UGA in 1940 as an instructor in zoology and, over his long career, pioneered the new fields of ecology and environmental science?

Eugene P. Odum

What native Georgian served as secretary of state in the Kennedy and Johnson administrations (1961–1969) and then taught international law at UGA from 1970 to 1992?

Dean Rusk

> "Nothing means more to a teacher than a student contacting them and saying, 'You meant something to me.'"
> —**Fred Stephenson**, author of *Extraordinary Teachers*

What six history professors, at the instigation of Governor Jimmy Carter, wrote *A History of Georgia* (1977) and presented the completed volume to President Carter at the White House in March 1978?

Numan V. Bartley, F.N. Boney, Kenneth Coleman, William F. Holmes, Phinizy Spalding and Charles E. Wynes

What recently-arrived professor is in the forefront of the scientific revolution called cloning?

Steven L. Stice

What professor won the Pulitzer Prize in History in 1998 for *Summer For the Gods: The Scopes Trial and America's Continuing Debate Over Science and Religion*?

Edward J. Larson

> "It's truly exciting to see the students suddenly understand this marvelous place—the Middle East."
> —**Eve Troutt Powell**, MacArthur Foundation Fellow

Is there a secret history of the foibles of the faculty?

No—fortunately

Faculty **35**

> "To me it was a privilege and an honor to attend the Georgia Law School and I owe it much and am grateful."
>
> —**Edith House, one of the first woman graduates, 1925**

Alumni

When was the alumni society formed and by whom?

1834 by Augustin S. Clayton (class of 1804)

What role did UGA play in the establishment of the Georgia Female College (now Wesleyan College), one of the first true women's colleges?

Its first president and founder was the Reverend George F. Pierce (class of 1829)

What graduate of the class of 1826 served as a justice of the U.S. Supreme Court from 1853 to 1861 and then served as assistant secretary of war for the Confederacy?

John A. Campbell

> "It was indeed a triumph over the racism that had ruled the day."
> —Charlayne Hunter-Gault reflecting on desegregation at the university

What local student, nicknamed "Fatty" and briefly expelled before graduating in 1834, became a famous Democratic politician, secretary of the treasury under President James Buchanan, and a Confederate general?

Howell Cobb

What prominent alumni played a major role in winning Georgia's support for the Compromise of 1850 that held the Union together for another decade?

Howell Cobb (class of 1834), Charles J. Jenkins (1820–1822), Alexander H. Stephens (class of 1832), and Robert Toombs (1824–1828)

At the state convention of January 1861, what prominent alumni favored and opposed the secession motion that passed by a narrow margin?

For secession: Henry L. Benning (class of 1834), Howell Cobb (class of 1834), Thomas R.R. Cobb (class of 1841), and Eugenius Aristides Nisbet (class of 1821)

Against secession: Herschel V. Johnson (class of 1834) and Alexander H. Stephens (class of 1832)

What member of the class of 1847 became a famous writer-humorist under the pen name "Bill Arp" during the Civil War?

Charles Henry Smith

What was UGA's enrollment when the Civil War erupted in 1861?

About one hundred

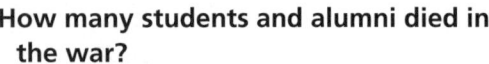

How many students and alumni died in the war?

About one hundred

A painting of what rebel general in full uniform, killed in action at Fredericksburg in 1862, hangs in the foyer of the main law school building?

Thomas R.R. Cobb (top graduate in the class of 1841 and one of the law school's founders)

How many regular students were in the class of 1861 and how many died in the war?

Twenty-two, six

Who was the Floridian who attended UGA in 1844, transferred to West Point, became an ordinance officer in the regular army, and served in that capacity in the Union army during the Civil War?

Stephen Vincent Benet

> "I threw like I sing. Very softly."
> —**Whisperin' Bill Anderson** on his days on the UGA baseball field

Who presented an oil painting of General Benet, in formal blue uniform, to UGA in 1933?

The poet Stephen Vincent Benet (his grandson)

Who was the artist and what happened to the painting?

Henri Royer of Paris, it remains on campus and is occasionally exhibited

Fort Benning is named for what alumnus?

Confederate General Henry L. Benning (top graduate of the class of 1834)

Fort Gordon is named for what alumnus?

General John B. Gordon (class of 1853)

What prewar military instruction had these two outstanding soldiers received at UGA?

None

William G. Delony (top man in the class of 1846), a battle-hardened colonel of cavalry, wrote his wife in Athens of the "fascination in danger which allures a soldier" in September 1864 and met what fate three weeks later?

He was badly wounded, captured, and died in a Union hospital in Washington, D.C.

What young student in the class of 1861, much like "Paul" in *All Quiet On the Western Front*, eagerly joined the rebel army when the war started, fought all the way to the end in the infantry, only to be killed at Appomattox on April 9, 1865, in the last charge of Lee's army?

Private James Hamilton McWhorter from Maxeys, Georgia

Who led this last charge?

General John B. Gordon

What member of the class of 1866, a Confederate veteran and native Athenian and longtime registrar of UGA, wrote three early books on Athens and UGA?

Augustus Longstreet Hull

What outstanding American historian began his publishing career at UGA where he received an A.B. in 1897 and an M.A. in 1899?

Ulrich Bonnell Phillips

Reversing the traditional flow, where did he conclude his distinguished career?

Yale

> "I didn't choose to be an artist, it chose me."
> —**Joni Mabe**

> "My life has been about circles completing themselves."
> —Photographer Jack Leigh

In what way did many UGA men, often the sons of Johnny Rebs, look and act like "bluebellies" at the end of the nineteenth century?

They served in the U.S. (Union) Army in the Spanish-American War of 1898, wearing the traditional blue uniform

What two Georgia heroes of the Spanish-American War studied briefly at UGA (1868 and 1874) before transferring to Annapolis and graduating (1877 and 1879) and becoming career naval officers?

Albon C. Hodgson (at Santiago) and Thomas M. Brumby (at Manila Bay)

Who was one of the early Jewish graduates in 1878 who, with his brother, established what prominent business in Athens?

Moses Gershon Michael, the Michael Brothers Department Store

Who was UGA's first Rhodes Scholar in 1904?

Robert Preston Brooks, later dean of the School of Commerce

Who graduated in the class of 1917 at eighteen and went on to become a vice president of Chase National Bank and then president of the International Bank for Reconstruction and Development in 1949?

Eugene R. Black Jr.

Who was the valedictorian of the class of 1917, captain of the cadet corps, the school's second Rhodes Scholar, an Episcopalian minister, and the first man in his division (now the 82nd Airborne) killed in action in France in June 1918?

Henry Lee Jewett Williams

What native of Winder served in the naval reserve while studying law (LL.B. 1918) and then as a U.S. senator served on the Naval Affairs and then Armed Forces Committees from 1933 to 1969, wielding great power?

Richard B. Russell Jr.

What graduate (A.B. 1893) first won fame as the successful prosecutor of Leo Frank in the sensational Mary Phegan murder case in 1913 and then was governor of Georgia from 1917 to 1921?

Hugh M. Dorsey

What graduate of the class of 1901 donated so much money to upgrading the law school that the new law building of 1932 was named in his honor?

Harold Hirsch

What famous Italian fashion designer attended UGA in 1935 and 1936?

Emilio Pucci

> "Good football teams still have to block and tackle, and Synovus has to live those fundamental values or we won't succeed."
> —**Jimmy Blanchard, Synovus CEO**

What did he study and where did he and some other foreign students live?

Agriculture, they lived on the top floor of Memorial Hall (before air conditioning)

What foreigners did UGA recognize as outstanding alumni in 1973?

Louis Deroche (France), Emilio Pucci (Italy) and Herbertus Scheibe (Germany)—they all attended UGA in the 1930s

Among the many Hodgsons who attended UGA, who (class of 1893) spearheaded many alumni fund drives over the years as a successful Athens businessman?

Harry Hodgson

> "Anyone fortunate enough to make their living in art should have a social responsibility of some kind."
> —Alan Campbell

What native Georgian and famous film comedian in the 1930–1950s claimed to have briefly attended the law school?

Oliver Hardy

What two alumni played major roles in establishing a central board of regents for all public higher education in Georgia?

Philip Weltner (A.B. 1907) and Hughes Spalding (LL.B. 1910)

Who was the first UGA man killed in action in World War II?

Lacy Mangleburg, flying over the Burma Road in January 1942

Who was UGA's first graduate (B.S. 1941) to receive the Congressional Medal of Honor in World War II?

Lt. Daniel Warnell Lee during the invasion of Southern France in 1944

> "The sun never sets on the University of Georgia."
> —**Carlton L. Curtis**

Who was the manager of the *Pandora* in 1954 who later became one of the best journalists at explaining the state's swirling politics?

Bill Shipp

What governor at the beginning of World War II meddled in UGA affairs enough to bring a brief loss of accreditation to the whole system of white colleges?

Eugene Talmadge (LL.B. 1906)

Who was his son, also an alumnus (LL.B. 1946), who generally was said to have done more financially for UGA than any previous governor?

Herman Talmadge, governor from 1948 to 1955

"Somewhere in there the music and the realness gets to cooking and brewing and it becomes just part of the stew."
—**Dave Schools, Widespread Panic**

What two former students worked on the Manhattan Project that produced the atomic bomb during World War II?

Francis G. Slack (B.S. 1918) and Eugene T. Booth Jr. (B.S. 1932 and M.S. 1934)

Who was the football lineman who graduated in 1952, became a leader of the Green Berets, compiled a brilliant combat record, and finally led the daring but unsuccessful raid to liberate hostages in Iran in 1980?

Colonel Charlie A. Beckwith

Who was the graduate in the class of 1924 from Tifton who prospered in the insurance business and over the years donated so many old books and manuscripts to the library that his name now prefixes the Rare Book and Manuscript Library?

Felix Hargrett

> "My father always told me to either work for the civil service or work for myself because everything else wasn't much fun."
>
> **—Thomas J. Stanley, author of *The Millionaire Next Door***

Of the last twenty-two governors of the state dating back to 1913, how many never attended UGA?

Five

What former editor of the *Red and Black* (1975–1976) won a Pulitzer Prize in 1992 for a series on animal research for the *Sacramento Bee*?

Deborah Blum

What alumnus, whose football career was ended by an injury in 1931, became a successful financier and in 1956 gave all 900 graduating seniors a share of stock in one of his corporations?

Louis Wolfson

> "So many of the relationships both in love and in life that I've been fortunate to have, have their roots at the University."
> —**Billy Payne**

Who allied with Jimmy Carter soon after graduating in 1967 and became a key advisor in Atlanta and Washington where he served as the president's chief of staff?

Hamilton Jordan

What journalism major in the 1960s emerged as UGA's most vocal homespun booster in recent years?

Lewis Grizzard

What was his classic rejoinder to newcomers who complained about his beloved state and beloved university?

"Delta is ready when you are"

What best-selling mystery writer attended UGA?

Stuart Woods

What governor of Georgia earned a doctorate in veterinary medicine from UGA?

Sonny Perdue

What two very generous benefactors, both natives of Macon, are honored by the splendid Ramsey Student Center for Physical Activities (1995) that was named by *Sports Illustrated* as "Best Student Recreation Center" in 1997?

> Bernard B. Ramsey (class of 1937) and his wife Eugenia A. Ramsey

What UGA alumnus wrote *The Millionaire Next Door*?

> Thomas J. Stanley

Who received a B.A. in 1965 and an M.A. in 1967 (both in English) and went on to become a leader at CNN and finally the president of the Public Broadcasting System?

> Pat Mitchell

> "You're always selling something, even if you're just selling yourself to another person."
> —**Dan Amos, AFLAC CEO**

> "People want the freedom to bake."
> —Anne Byrn, author of *The Cake Mix Doctor*

What popular singer attended UGA's Lamar Dodd School of Art?

Michael Stipe

Who graduated in 1970 with an A.B. and for seven years was the very successful top editor at *Fortune* and now has become editorial director of Time Inc. (the whole publishing empire and not just *Fortune* or *Time*)?

John Huey (who took an English class taught by Pat Mitchell)

What UGA graduate is listed in the *Guiness Book of World Records* for owning Elvis's wart?

Joni Mabe

Which *Survivor* contestant (first season) attended UGA?

Colleen Haskell

> "It's all about people."
> —Dink NeSmith, President, UGA Alumni Association

> "I just assumed when I was in high school that if you went to college, you went to the University of Georgia."
>
> —**Roy Barnes**

Leaders

Who wrote the charter of UGA in 1785 and was also its first president?

Abraham Baldwin (Yale 1772)

Who was the second president who actually started the school and ran it from 1801 to 1811?

Josiah Meigs (Yale 1778)

What role did one of his grandsons play in the Civil War?

Born in 1816 in Augusta where his father practiced medicine, Montgomery C. Meigs graduated from West Point in 1836, and during the war he was the outstanding quartermaster general of the entire Union army—just the kind of talent the Confederacy needed

> "Leadership is helping others achieve more than they ever thought they could."
> —J. W. Fanning

Influenced by his friend, Thomas Jefferson, what area of studies did Meigs stress more than most early college leaders?

Science

Who became president in 1819 and revived UGA that had almost faded away?

Moses Waddel

On his arrival in 1819, how did he describe UGA?

"I found the College nearly extinct, consisting of only seven students with three professors"

Before coming, what bright emerging politicos had he tutored?

William H. Crawford and John C. Calhoun

Who led UGA for the longest period, by far, of anyone?

Alonzo Church (1829–1859)

Was President Church also a Northerner?

Yes, a native of Vermont and a graduate of Middlebury College

What five reasons did students have to look forward to an invitation to dinner at the home of stern, puritanical President Church?

His five attractive daughters Elvira, Sarah Jane, Anna, Elizabeth, and Julia

What leader, the first chancellor in the reorganization of 1859, pushed to modernize the old school but then spent the next fourteen years struggling to keep UGA alive?

Andrew A. Lipscomb

> "Knowledge is more of a process than a destination."
> —**Zell Miller**

> "The University of Georgia—struggling against prejudice and illiberality—may its usefulness yet defeat the views of malignity."
>
> —President Josiah Meigs

What was his salary in Confederate money at the beginning of the Civil War?

$250

Who was the first native Georgian to lead UGA?

Chancellor Henry H. Tucker from Hancock County (1874–1878)

From 1811 to 1899 what was the profession of all of the school's leaders?

Protestant minister

For how long did Calvinistic Presbyterians control UGA?

Forty years, Moses Waddel 1819–1829 and Alonzo Church 1829–1859

Which chancellor (1888–1889) was a native of India (the child of Presbyterian missionaries) and a chaplain in the Confederate army?

William E. Boggs

> "History is a major part of where we're going."
> —**Maurice Daniels**

Who was the first non-minister to lead UGA in almost a century and the first alumnus ever to lead the school?

Walter B. Hill, a wealthy Macon lawyer (B.A. 1870 and B.L. 1871)

What was his main mission during his six-year administration?

To remake the old college into a modern university

When Chancellor Hill began his reforms, what school was his main model?

The University of Wisconsin at Madison

What native Georgian made a fortune as a financier in New York City late in the nineteenth century and became UGA's most generous benefactor?

George Foster Peabody

What wealthy northeasterner left provisions in his will in 1869 for education in the impoverished South that led to the building of Peabody Hall (1913) on the old north campus?

George Peabody (not George Foster Peabody)

What Wesleyan graduate received the first advanced degree awarded to a woman at UGA (an M.A.) in 1914 and what position did she soon hold at UGA?

Mary D. Lyndon, first dean of women

What V.M.I. graduate came to UGA in 1886, taught mathematics, led the cadet corps and served as dean, chancellor of UGA and finally chancellor of the new state university system from 1932–1933?

Charles M. Snelling

In the twentieth century what two leaders had the longest terms in office?

David C. Barrow, 1906–1925, and Fred C. Davison, 1967–1986

In the twentieth century what two leaders had the shortest terms in office?

Jonathan Clark Rogers, 1949–1950, and Henry King Stanford, 1986–1987

What was A & M College President Andrew M. Soule's "College on Wheels" in the early twentieth century?

A special train chartered to tour the state annually to demonstrate how the school served agrarian Georgia

"Your education and your future starts right here, as you pass this Arch."

—Dean William Tate

As UGA grew rapidly after World War II, who was the last administrator to be a traditional campus character, widely known and respected by the students?

Dean William Tate who retired in 1971

As an undergraduate in the early 1920s, what sport did he excel in?

Distance running, one and two miles, and cross country

Who came from Mercer in 1903 to teach English and for over forty-two years held almost every imaginable administrative post including chairman of the athletic committee, dean, president and chancellor of the entire state university system?

Steadman V. Sanford

> "If you want wealth to come out, you've got to put it in."
> —**Senator Phil Gramm**

Who graduated in 1919, got a law degree at Harvard, led UGA from 1935–1948 where he pushed a massive building program and finally served as chancellor of the entire state university system from 1948 to 1964?

Harmon W. Caldwell

What dean of the veterinary medicine school later became president of UGA?

Fred C. Davison

Who was the campus planning director from 1962 to 1981, a period of explosive growth?

William E. "Billy" Hudson

> "My mother used to repeat an old saying that if you have two loaves of bread, sell one and buy hyacinths. That's the way I feel about the mind and the spirit, where the humanities reside."
>
> **—State Representative Louise McBee**

What president of UGA from 1987 to 1997 directed a massive construction program capped off with the entire new east campus?

Charles B. Knapp

Before becoming president of UGA in 1997, what school did Michael F. Adams lead?

Centre College in Kentucky

> "If you dial heaven from Athens, it's a local call."
> —**Athens Area Chamber of Commerce**

Town-gown

What was the original name of the tiny settlement where UGA was placed?

Cedar Shoals

Who owned the small mill at Cedar Shoals and pushed hard for it to be the site of UGA?

Daniel Easley

When did the name change from Cedar Shoals to Athens?

1801

When was the earliest map or plat made?

1805

> "Malaga, Madeira, Teneriffe, Muscatelle, Cherry-Bounce, Shrub, Claret—and Porter"
>
> —**Athens liquor shop sign, 1830s**

What family names claimed the most of the twenty-four town lots?

Phinizy (four), Morris (three), Allan (three) and Cary (two)

What are a few town-gown names that have persisted through UGA's history?

Barrow, Cobb, Hodgson, and McWhorter

Reflecting the early frontier days of UGA, what does the sheriff still carry in the commencement procession?

A sword

Generally, early Athenians were praised for what traits?

Gentility and hospitality

However, some visitors mentioned what less flattering traits?

Ostentation and family pretension

When did Georgia's rapidly expanding railroad system reach Athens?

1841

Briefly, what was the means of propulsion?

Horses

What was the original name of Broad Street?

Front Street

Slave workers were occasionally hired by the year for about what amount?

$100

> "This [Athens] is a literary town."
> —Samuel J. Flynt, 19 May 1860

What was the female preparatory school established in Athens in 1858 and absorbed into UGA in the 1930s?

Lucy Cobb Institute

A statue of what graced its grounds?

A goat

Who were the two favorite black bell ringers on campus in the antebellum period?

Old Dick Corly and Blenham

In 1860 what was the population of Athens and what percentage were black slaves?

Almost 4,000 and half were slaves

In 1860 what was the enrollment at UGA?

100

> "His [Lamar Dodd's] absolute conviction that the visual arts were important—not only as a discipline, but for their effect on the general public—transformed Athens."
> **—William U. Eiland**

What unsuccessful weapon was manufactured at the Athens Foundry during the Civil War, and where is it now?

A doubled-barreled cannon now located on the lawn of the City Hall

What did General Sherman's army do to UGA and Athens?

Nothing—Sherman's troops passed through Madison, twenty miles to the south, heading southeast toward Savannah and Madison emerged virtually unscathed too

In August 1864 a clash between Athens home guards and some Union cavalry occurred at Barber's Creek and resulted in how many deaths?

None on either side as the Yankees pulled back and headed toward capture near Winder

> "[Athens] was a college town where culture and refinement must be bred and developed—it would be called the 'Classic City.'"
>
> —E. Merton Coulter, *College Life in the Old South*

When did Union troops occupy UGA?

At the end of the war, briefly

What were most of the school's meager funds invested in during the Civil War?

Confederate bonds

What were they worth at the end of the war?

Nothing

When did Athens replace Watkinsville as the seat of Clarke County and when did Watkinsville become the seat of new Oconee County, carved out of southwestern Clarke County?

1871, 1875

What two major gifts did the town of Athens make to UGA?

In 1874 $25,000 for Moore College and in 1905 $20,000 to purchase 500 acres for the new south campus

Who was the Athenian who persuaded his town to put up $25,000 for the new building?

Richard Moore, a physician and member of UGA's board of trustees

Who was the Athens area's most unreconstructed rebel after the Civil War?

Amidst strong competition, Miss Mildred Lewis ("Millie") Rutherford

When did the Athens area feel the vibrations of a devastating earthquake centered near Charleston, South Carolina?

1886

Who was the old blind African American man, born a slave, who was well known on campus until his death in 1901?

Lewis Green ("Old Tub")

Where was the first garden club in America organized?

Athens in 1891

The Garden Club of Georgia evolved from this beginning and has had what two locations at UGA?

From 1938 to 1998 the Founders Memorial Garden and antebellum faculty house on the north campus and after 1998 the magnificent new headquarters building at the State Botanical Garden

What professor championed this project on campus?

Hubert B. Owens, later dean of the School of Environmental Design

In round numbers what was the population of Athens in 1900? Of UGA?

10,000; 300

> "The wise person does not ask how soon can I finish my education, but how long may I continue to grow."
> —**Chancellor David C. Barrow**

What did David C. Barrow do after he learned he had been designated the new chancellor of UGA?

Announced "Coca-Cola for everyone!" to an assemblage of students in Costa's soda fountain in the Southern Mutual Building

When Chancellor David C. Barrow ran UGA from 1905–1925, before the huge growth of administration, who served as his only secretary for many years?

Sarah Cobb Baxter

What were some favorite town spots for students in the 1930s?

Costa's Ice Cream Parlor, the Palace Theatre and Patrick's Drug Store

"When Margie and Phinizy Spalding moved to Hill Street in the 1970s, they began a renaissance of 'Athens' first suburb,' Cobbham . . ."

—**Milton Leathers**

What local photographer recorded the town-gown scene from the 1930s through the 1970s?

Kenneth Kay

The original burial ground for Athens and UGA remains partially intact where?

On Jackson Street between Baldwin Hall (1938) and the Visual Arts Building (1961)

According to rumor, what was dug up and hauled away with the normal dirt during the construction of Baldwin Hall in the late 1930s?

Bones

After World War II what famous literary figure visited his friend Professor Hugh Hodgson every year and delivered increasingly popular lectures on campus?

Robert Frost

What famous author lived with his mother's family in Athens after his father's suicide in 1930?

Walker Percy

What two similarly named but dissimilarly operated businesses served the community until the late 1970s?

Essie's served Southern cooking on Broad Street, and Effie's served Southern "luv" on Elm Street

When did the U.S. Navy Supply Corps School move into an area of North Athens that used to be part of UGA?

1954

Some fine old homes on Milledge Avenue were saved by whom?

Fraternities and sororities

What Georgia politician flipped burgers at Allen's Hamburgers, a restaurant and bar featuring the "Coldest Beer in Town?"

Zell Miller

What fast-food restaurant at the corner of College Avenue and Broad Street served the community from 1933 to 1978?

The Varsity

The original of this restaurant served what community?

Georgia Tech and Atlanta

What weekly town journal covers the booming music scene and related arts in Athens?

Flagpole

What has recently proliferated on campus and downtown?

Computers and bars

In 2000 what was the enrollment at UGA and the total population of metropolitan Athens (Clarke, Oconee and Madison Counties)?

31,288; 153,444 (including students)

What natural phenomenon plagued the area as a new century dawned?

Drought

How many different venues has the world-famous 40 Watt Club been located in?

Five different venues—College Street, corner of College and Broad, twice on Clayton Street, Broad Street, and now its current location on Washington Street

> "[Athens] is the most beautiful town I have seen on my journey so far, and the only one in the South that I would like to revisit."
>
> —**John Muir, 1867**

What restaurant's slogan became world-famous after the release of R.E.M.'s *Automatic for the People*?

Weaver D's

How many people attended the Widespread Panic CD release party in downtown Athens on April 18, 1998?

About 100,000

What "college movie" was filmed in Athens?

Road Trip

What television series was filmed in Athens?

Breaking Away

What Athens landmark was willed eight feet of land around its base and was recognized by Ripley's Believe It or Not?

The tree that owns itself

"[Athens] is really an incredible place."
—**Michael Stipe**

> "I think about what I can do to enhance—whether it's the School of Music, the University, or the community . . ."
> —**Arvin Scott**

What band who began in Athens sings about "heading down the Atlanta Highway"?

B-52's

What sport drew about 30,000 people to downtown Athens in April of 2001, and what was the name of the race?

Bike racing, Xcelerate Twilight—the 22nd annual Twilight Criterium

What author who resides in Athens became the best-selling author in Japan in 2001?

Terry Kay

> "A college or seminary of learning."
> —State law 1784

Government

What was the original method the state used to finance the new university?

Land grants

Who donated the original 633-acre plot for the new school?

John Milledge

What kind of location did the founders seek?

Isolated and rural, far from the distractions of cities

What nearby villages were considered?

Watkinsville and Greensboro

> "We can confidently rely upon the annual overflowings of this Georgia Nile for the fertilization of our rising country."
>
> —**Senatus Academicus Minutes, 1825**

The original Board of Trustees and Board of Visitors combined under what stilted title?

Senatus Academicus

What was the first chartered state university in America?

The University of Georgia in 1785

What other school also claims to be number one?

The University of North Carolina at Chapel Hill, chartered in 1789 and classes began in 1795

When did UGA actually begin classes?

1801

Who was the first American president to visit UGA while in office?

James Monroe on 21 May 1819, during a tour of the South

How did the title of the leader of UGA change over time?

President from 1785 to 1859 and from 1931 to the present, Chancellor from 1859 to 1931

For over a century what group of local residents (and trustees) helped with day-to-day supervision of the school?

The Prudential Committee

Until 1870 for four dollars what could any graduate who had been out of school for three years (and stayed out of jail) receive from UGA?

A Master of Arts degree

In the 1850s how many schools in Georgia called themselves colleges and how many really were?

25 and 5: UGA (1785), Emory (1836), Mercer (1837), Oglethorpe (1838) and Wesleyan (1836), which with pretty good documentation claims to be the first real woman's college in America and the world—and presumably the galaxy

By the late 1850s the state had more money to appropriate to UGA because of what profitable economic activity?

Ownership of the Western and Atlantic Railroad from Atlanta to Chattanooga

What previous college work was required for admission to the early law school founded in 1859 and how long was the course of study?

None, one year

When were graduations held before the Civil War and how long did they last?

Early August, 3 to 4 days (and nights)

> "A damned pack or band of Tories and speculators"
> —**President Josiah Meigs on the Trustees 1809**

What happened in 1872 to reinvigorate poverty-stricken UGA?

UGA became a federal land grant college eligible for federal financial support

What odd situation did this create?

Northerners were hated, but Northern dollars were loved

Joseph E. Brown, Georgia's famous secessionist and Civil War governor, attended what college and made what contribution to UGA in 1882?

Yale, a $50,000 scholarship fund for students at UGA

> "Freedom is worth its cost."
> —Chancellor David C. Barrow, 1917

According to the college *Bulletin* in 1908, what was the cost of tuition?

Nothing—with $2 a month dormitory rent, $9 a month for meals at the student dining hall, and an annual library fee of $5

President-elect William Howard Taft was persuaded to come from Augusta to Athens in mid-January 1901 partly because of what old school tie?

He was a graduate of Yale, UGA's parent school

When was the present centralized system of public higher education under a single Board of Regents and Chancellor instituted, and who was the "boy wonder" governor who directed this and the reorganization of the entire state government?

1931 by Richard B. Russell Jr. (LL.B. 1918)

What program, begun in 1918 and discontinued in 1933, was revived in 1946 and now flourishes?

Veterinary medicine

> "Let us erect a university, a real university, a university in fact as well as name."
> —**Chancellor Charles M. Snelling, 1925**

From 1972 to 1992 what was required to get a name on the wall in the President's Club Garden on the south side of Old College?

A gift of $10,000 to UGA

What vast photographic collection at the State Archives in Atlanta contains many photos of Athens and UGA?

Vanishing Georgia

During the bicentennial celebration who delivered the main address on October 1, 1984?

Vice President George Bush (a graduate of Yale)

Although technically a branch of UGA at times, the Medical College of Georgia has always been located where?

Augusta

> "We will ensure that the University of Georgia is always a place of hope and vision."
> —**President Michael F. Adams**

What is the new name of the traditional home economics operation?

College of Family and Consumer Sciences

When was the Coca-Cola Masters in Marketing Program established within the Terry College of Business?

1986

What major academic switch began in 1998?

The change from four quarters per year to three semesters per year

What national awards are presented annually in New York City by the Henry W. Grady College of Journalism and Mass Communication?

The George Foster Peabody awards for excellence in radio and television

"...arguably the fastest-rising public university in the country."
Fiske Guide to Colleges

> "The university in the twentieth century will be differentiated from its predecessors in this: It will connect its activities more closely with the business and life of the people . . ."
> —**Chancellor Walter B. Hill, 1905**

What is the one-word designation of the recent lottery-funded tuition and books scholarships for Georgians who maintain a B average and what governor established this popular program?

HOPE by Zell Miller (A.B. 1957 and M.A. 1958 at UGA)

Where are the main overseas programs operated by UGA?

Avignon in France, Oxford in England, Cortona and Verona in Italy and Valencia and Cadiz in Spain

Where was University System Chancellor Stephen R. Portch (1994–2001) from, originally and most recently, before coming to Georgia?

England, Wisconsin

> "The condition of the garden wears somewhat the aspect of being neglected..."
> —**William Gilmore Simms in 1849 in *Charleston Newspaper***

Buildings and Grounds

What was UGA's (and the area's) first permanent building?

Old College (1806)

What older building was it modeled after?

Connecticut Hall at Yale

What was the original name of Old College and indeed the name unofficially applied to the whole school often in the nineteenth century?

Franklin College

It was named in honor of whom?

Benjamin Franklin, a lobbyist for Georgia in the colonial period, a Revolutionary hero and a self-made scientist with an international reputation

> "Soule Hall . . . that should keep those coeds off the streets and in their rooms where they belong."
> —*Pandora* 1975

In the first plat or map of 1804 what three campus buildings are shown?

Old College, the President's house (wooden) and the Grammar School (wooden)

What four-story, dormitory-classroom building was finished in 1823 as the third old campus structure, but burned to the ground in 1830 and was rebuilt in 1832 with three stories?

New College

What is the second oldest building on campus and one of the most overlooked?

Philosophical Hall (1821), now called Waddel Hall

What happened to the original botanical garden established near UGA in 1831?

It was sold in 1856 to raise funds to construct the iron fence and Arch

When were the Arch and the fence erected?

1858

What happened to the Arch's gate?

Nobody knows, but it disappeared long before athletic rivalries led to campus raids

Where does the best detailed illustration of the antebellum campus appear?

Gleason's Magazine in 1854

Where does another detailed illustration of the antebellum campus appear?

In 1859, on the border of James R. Butts's large map of Georgia

What two church denominations had buildings on campus before the Civil War?

Baptists and Presbyterians

The antebellum Greek revival mansion on Prince Avenue built in 1856 by John T. Grant (an alumnus and railroad builder) and restored after World War II now serves UGA in what capacity?

Home of the President

Where was the law school housed in its early days before the Civil War?

At the law office of Thomas R.R. Cobb and Joseph Henry Lumpkin off campus on the corner of Prince and Pulaski (at the present location of Saint Joseph's Church)

Where were most of the books located on campus in 1850?

The two literary societies had 5,000 and the school library contained 1,400

> "The Coliseum—labeled by one of our coeds 'as ugly as a pregnant oyster.'"
> —*Pandora* 1973

What artist left the school a fine landscape painting of distant Athens and UGA in the 1840s?

George Cooke

What is probably the most significant (and expensive) American manuscript housed in the Hargrett Rare Book and Manuscript Library?

The original Confederate Constitution of 1861

What were the main uses of the new campus building bordering on Broad Street completed as the Civil War began?

Museum of natural history on the third floor, library on the second floor, and a lecture hall holding up to three hundred people on the first floor

What happened to it in 1905?

It was joined with the nearby enlarged Ivy Building by rooms in the back and a Corinthian portico in the front to become the Academic Building

What further name change occurred in 2001?

It was renamed the Holmes/Hunter Academic Building in honor of the first two African American students who registered for classes there in January 1961

University High School in North Athens and later the State Normal School both used a building constructed in 1862 that was informally known as what?

Rock College (or more formally Gilmer Hall by the Normal School)

What was the campus headquarters of the Union troops who arrived in Athens in May 1865?

Phi Kappa Hall

What building in town by the river housed the Cook Brothers Armory during the Civil War, later became a textile mill and finally in the 1980s was absorbed by UGA?

The Chicopee Building

What is the name of the huge painting at the rear of the Chapel, who painted it, and who gave it to UGA in 1867?

The Interior of Saint Peter's was painted by George Cooke, and it was a gift from Alabama industrialist Daniel Pratt

What happened to it in 1955?

It was badly damaged by fire, and it took local artist Walter Frobos and his daughter eighteen months to restore it, mount it on masonite and frame it in redwood

"One of the greatest college towns in America."

—Adam Gross, landscape architect

> "Why is the University of Georgia so beautiful in comparison to us?"
>
> —University of Virginia president John Casteen upon returning from visit to UGA

What new building was constructed in 1874 to fulfill the obligation of a federal land grant college?

Moore College

When did New College stop being a dormitory and become entirely a classroom building?

1889

On the old north campus what building replaced Science Hall, built in 1897 and burned to the ground in 1903, and what valuable papers were lost in the fire?

Terrell Hall (1904) on the same site but two stories instead of three, and many of Chancellor Walter B. Hill's official papers were lost in the fire

Which of the original buildings, known as "Yahoo Hall" by the beginning of the twentieth century, was almost demolished as UGA began to modernize?

Old College

What was the first major building on the new south campus, and who was it named for?

Conner Hall (1908) in honor of state legislator James J. Conner, a champion of agricultural education

What was its original name?

Agricultural Hall

What older home (1844) crowds up against Conner Hall and who originally owned it?

The Lumpkin House, sometimes called the Rock House, and it was built by Governor Wilson Lumpkin (1831–1835) who championed Cherokee removal

What is unusual about the 1907 deed of sale transferring the house and lot to UGA?

A provision that the property would revert to the Lumpkin family if the house was ever removed

This new south campus that emerged early in the twentieth century was originally devoted to what field?

Agriculture

What is its general emphasis now?

Science and technology

Where was the cadet corps armory from 1872 on into the twentieth century?

The Ivy Building (now the south wing of the Academic Building)

The northeast corner of the original north campus (at the corner of Broad and Jackson Streets) has remained open, but early in the twentieth century what was located there?

Tennis courts

When did the literary societies turn over their library books to UGA, and what department housed them for awhile?

Around 1890 when the history department took control of them

What happened to the tall cupola with a bell that sat on the front roof of the Chapel?

It was removed in 1913 because it was near collapse, and the bell was transferred to a new tower at the back of the Chapel

> "Here in Athens, the tourist can say, this is the South I have read about."
> —**Hal Steed, 1942**

When does it ring?

It heralds major athletic victories—and presumably the successful conclusion of atomic warfare

Until the twentieth century where were most graduations held?

The Chapel

What building was unofficially known as "the co-ed barn" when it was completed in 1920?

Soule Hall, the first women's dormitory

Where was the law school located from 1919 to 1932?

Across Broad Street from the old campus in the Athenaeum Building (later demolished)

What does Memorial Hall (1925) memorialize?

The forty-seven UGA men who died in World War I

> "[The UGA campus] is shaped like a sausage that's been extruded over the years."
>
> —**Dexter Adams, University of Georgia Landscape Architect**

What was the name of the large, wooden, "temporary," one-story building constructed around 1916 on the site of the present parking lot beside the main library and finally torn down just before World War II?

The Octagon

Name some of the main buildings constructed with federal funds in 1938–1939.

Baldwin, LeConte, Park, Rutherford, and Snelling Halls and the Forest Resources Building

In the 1930s what was grounds foreman Oscar Winemiller's technique for discouraging illegal parking around campus buildings?

He deflated the offending automobile's tires

> "It's almost like two separate universities."
> —University of Georgia Student, referring to the differences between north and south campus

What happened to scenic Lake Kirota and the wooden dormitory called Camp Wilkins after World War II?

They were removed to make way for the College of Veterinary Medicine and other modern expansion

When did the U.S. Navy operate a massive pre-flight training program on campus (one of only five in the nation)?

During World War II from June 1942 to mid-1945

What was the U.S. Navy's designation of some of the buildings used for the preflight program?

Old College was Ranger Barracks, Rutherford Hall was Langley Barracks, Milledge Hall was Wasp Barracks and Baldwin Hall was the Operations Building

Which of these buildings did the U.S. Navy drastically restructure and improve inside without any outside additions?

Old College

To what two buildings did the U.S. Navy construct significant additions?

Baldwin Hall and Memorial Hall

What was the most feared and disliked aspect of the U.S. Navy's three-month training program?

The obstacle course

What two buildings constructed by the U.S. Navy in 1943 were demolished recently?

Stegeman Hall in 1995 and the Alumni House (originally a field house) in 2001

What was the name of the separate campus for freshman and sophomore women operated by UGA from 1933 to 1953, and where was it located?

The Coordinate Campus was in North Athens at the present site of the Navy Supply Corps School

Before the Science Center was completed on the south campus in 1959–1960, where was the Physics Department jammed in?

Moore College

Where was the School of Pharmacy, established in 1903, housed?

Terrell Hall and New College and finally in 1964 the Pharmacy Building on the south campus

Before and after World War II where was the campus snack bar located and what was it called?

On the first floor of New College, the Co-op

The will of Ilah Dunlap Little left $400,000 for the construction of what building completed in 1953?

The main library

What old building, completed in 1849, was torn down to make way for this new facility?

The Chancellor's House

What was the famous iron horse that briefly graced the campus in 1954?

It was a modernistic, metal sculpture that drew protests and even assaults from students, so it was banished to a farm in nearby Greene County where it still stands defiantly

What did the Russians do to encourage the construction of the six-building Science Center, completed in 1960?

In 1957 they orbited Sputnik and panicked the American scientific and political community

What was the greatest "might have been" federally-financed construction project that was rejected at the last moment by conservative Governor Lester Maddox?

An elaborate overhead monorail system to connect the north and south campuses that was then built at West Virginia University in Morgantown

> "The soul of the University resides [on north campus]."
>
> **—President Michael F. Adams**

Buildings and Grounds **107**

> "How do I get to the McDonald's in downtown Athens?"
>
> —Visitor to the university, after being told to meet friends at the Arch

What building, once described as a "pregnant oyster," was completed in 1964, finally giving UGA an adequate arena for basketball, concerts and other activities before large audiences?

Stegeman Coliseum

What happened to the open-air amphitheater completed in 1922 on the south campus?

It was replaced by the Boyd Graduate Studies Center in 1967

What large south campus building was massively renovated and rededicated in 1976?

Conner Hall

Old Moore College has housed what operations since World War II?

Physics, then Romance Languages and finally, in 2001, the honors program

In the 1981–1983 period what threat led to renovations in eight dormitories?

Asbestos

What mansion, built in 1894, dominated a mill town near Athens and was eventually given to UGA and restored by the School of Forest Resources?

White Hall

What dramatic expansion of the continuous campus occurred in the 1990s?

The large new east campus

What areas of study or disciplines does it stress?

Music, art and physical education

What state-of-the-art auditorium seating 1,100 is the main attraction within the new Performing Arts Center on this new campus?

Hodgson Hall

The Georgia General Assembly has designated which three UGA operations as official state institutions?

The Botanical Garden, the Georgia Museum of Art, and the Museum of Natural History

What building about a mile away from campus became in 1985 the most dramatically modern structure in the area?

The Alice Hand Callaway Visitor Center and Conservatory at the State Botanical Garden of Georgia

Funded by the W.K. Kellogg Foundation and the state, originally built in 1956 and vastly expanded since, what campus complex pushed education beyond the usual classroom-dormitory experience?

The Georgia Center for Continuing Education

> "Time Discloseth All Things."
> —Fresco in the front entrance to Brooks Hall, where murals painted in the 1940s were discovered after the fire in 1995

What often overlooked old building (1905) briefly held the office of former Governor Zell Miller before he became a U.S. Senator in 2000, and what was its original name?

Meigs Hall, originally LeConte Hall

Where was the large exhibition commemorating UGA over two centuries displayed in the bicentennial year of 1985, and what is there now?

The main floor of Memorial Hall, now the faculty dining hall

In August 1995 what splendid building, designed by Neel Reid and completed in 1928, caught fire while being repaired and was not fully repaired until January 1997?

Brooks Hall

What new breed of massive, plain, box-like structures have recently emerged on campus, and where is the most attractive one located?

Parking decks, with the new one completed in 2001 beside the Coliseum giving promise of better designs to come

What area of UGA operations has taken over most of the original old north campus?

Administration

What campus buildings are the most difficult to find one's way around in?

The Life Sciences Building, with Memorial Hall a close second

What Australian company with four of the sixty-four embryonic stem cell lines President Bush approved for federally-funded research has an office on campus?

BresaGen Limited

Where should people go to be introduced to UGA and to arrange a guided tour of the campus?

The Visitors Center on the east campus

What is the name of the library housing rare books and manuscripts that is located on the third floor of the main library?

The Hargrett Rare Book and Manuscript Library

Where is the impressive but largely unknown Georgia Museum of Natural History located?

In the Statistics Building on the south campus and in six other scattered campus buildings

> "I think that this is the beginning of some good changes on campus."
>
> **—UGA student, referring to the replacement of the parking lot on former Herty Field with a fountain**

What are the largest and smallest specimens in its vast collections?

A complete right whale skeleton and *coccidiasus legeri*, a single-cell yeast-like parasite that inhabits the gut of a fruit fly

> "Prince Charles will drop in on the GA-KY game Saturday to see what these yanks do with their weekends."
>
> —*Columns*
> **17 October 1977**

Sports

Before the Civil War what organized athletic teams did UGA support?

None

Who was UGA's first football opponent on 30 January 1892?

Mercer, which was crushed 50 to 0

When did the Tech-Georgia rivalry begin, and who won this game?

November 1893 in a football game in Athens that ended 28 to 6 (never mind who won)

> "I bleed Red and Black!"
> —**Vince Dooley**

In this first epic clash what did the teams call themselves?

The Georgia Wildcats and the Tech Blacksmiths

Who starred for Georgia Tech in this game?

Lt. Leonard Wood who was a U.S. Army doctor stationed at Fort McPherson in Atlanta

Where did similar UGA "ringers" usually enroll?

The law school

Who were some "far out" football opponents over the years?

The Augusta Athletic Club (1893–1894), the Atlanta Athletic Club (1898), the Savannah Athletic Club (1893–1894 and 1906), Locust Grove (1910), Alabama Presbyterian (1911 and 1913), and Daniel Field (military in Augusta, 1943–1944)

Which two of these teams actually defeated UGA and which team took the worst beating?

The Savannah Athletic Club won 12-0 in 1906 and Daniel Field won 18-7 in 1943, while Locust Grove was clobbered 101-0 in 1910

> "If there is a chance to win, you can do it if you believe and don't let up."
> —Herschel Walker

> "Once I visited Athens, I made it my home for life."
> —**Frank Sinkwich**

What UGA football player was killed in a football game in 1897, and who successfully appealed to the governor not to sign a bill outlawing the game in the state?

Von Gammom, his mother

Who coached the football team in 1895–1896, then moved to Carlile and coached Jim Thorp and later fielded powerful teams at Pittsburgh and Stanford to win national fame?

Glenn S. "Pop" Warner

Where were early football and baseball games played on campus from 1892 to 1911?

In the open area west of New College and south of Moore College

What was the main athletic area from 1912 until the opening of the modern stadium in 1929?

Sanford Field located southeast of the intersection of Lumpkin and Baxter Streets

> "I'm gonna play in the Rose Bowl."
> —**Bob Poss, 1942**

What became a popular new intramural sport early in the twentieth century?

Pushball

What was the first mascot of the early athletic teams?

A goat

Originally what were the school's athletic colors?

Red, black and gold, but gold was soon dropped when some protested that yellow implied cowardice and would be more appropriate elsewhere

118 The University of Georgia Trivia Book

Why do UGA football players wear helmets featuring a black "G" with white stripes?

In 1964, Vince Dooley designed this helmet because he was impressed with the look of the Green Bay Packers' helmets

On the mediocre football team of 1903, who were the smallest and largest players?

Back Harry "Kid" Woodruff (120 pounds from Columbus) and lineman G.A. "Baby" Moore (275 pounds from Greensboro)

Who was the sports writer who revealed UGA's use of "ringers" against Georgia Tech in the 1907 game?

Grantland Rice of the *Nashville Tennessean*

> "You know, Dan, life can be truly glorious when you are leading Georgia Tech on Grant Field, 21-0, at halftime."
>
> —**Bill Munday to Dan Magill, 1959**

What were the repercussions?

UGA Coach W.S. "Bull" Whitney resigned immediately, and in 1908, for the first time in six seasons, no game was played against Tech

What running back was UGA's first All-American in 1913?

Bob McWhorter

In what two years did UGA suspend football and why?

1917–1918 because of World War I

When did the intense Georgia-Tech rivalry lead to a six-year suspension of the football game?

1919–1924

What caused this rivalry to boil over uncontrollably?

At the 1919 senior parade in Athens two floats indicated that Tech men stayed behind to play football while UGA men fought heroically in France during World War I

> *"Get after their anatomy."*
> **—Erk Russell**

What was the name of UGA's first dog mascot, a female bull terrier who came to the campus in 1894 and reigned for many years?

Trilby

Who starred in football and captained the 1911 team, prospered in business in Columbus, and from 1923 to 1927 was UGA's only $1 a year football coach while compiling a 32-16-1 record?

George "Kid" Woodruff

What football and baseball star in the class of 1933 became one of baseball's top pitchers with the mighty New York Yankees?

Spurgeon "Spud" Chandler

> "The word *bulldog* first crept into the Georgia literature in 1901..."
> —John Stegeman

When was the present football stadium originally constructed, what was its seating capacity, and what is it now?

1929 with a seating capacity of 33,000, now 92,020

Who did much of the original construction work?

Convicts

What school accepted the honor of coming to Athens to inaugurate the new stadium?

Yale

Who won and who was the star?

The Georgia Bulldogs defeated the Yale Bulldogs 15 to 0 with All-American end Vernon "Catfish" Smith scoring all of the points

When did the series with Yale begin?

1923 with a Yale win 40-0 in New Haven

> "College games are as characteristic of this age as the Olympic games were of the age of Pindar."
>
> —**Dr. Steadman V. Sanford, 1929**

When did UGA first defeat Yale?

1927 in New Haven by a score of 14 to 10

In October 1931, after a convincing UGA win in New Haven by a score of 26 to 7, how did a *New York Sun* reporter describe the victors, what did the Yale marching band play at the end of the game, and how did the small number of UGA fans respond?

"Soft-tongued cracker warriors," "Dixie," the rebel yell

How did the reporter describe the yell?

". . . that blood-chilling shriek. . . . It's a sound you can't forget."

When did the series end?

1934, with a UGA win 14 to 7 in New Haven

How did the series stand when it ended?

Yale five wins (1923–26 and 1928); UGA six wins (1927 and 1929–1934)

What are two unusual features of UGA's football stadium?

Former bulldog mascots are buried there, and Tanyard Branch (a creek) runs in a tunnel under the south stands

What are two false rumors about the stadium?

Unsuccessful football coaches are also buried there, and Clemson, South Carolina and Auburn fans are often found wandering around in the tunnel which they mistake for a latrine ("look, Maybell, just like home!")

What happened to the football team of 1931 that traveled by train to California with an 8-1 record, got the grand tour of Hollywood and then played the University of Southern California?

They got slaughtered 60 to 0!

> "When I hear somebody say something against Georgia, I won't put up with it."
> —Spec Towns

Who were some of the Hollywood stars who distracted the UGA players?

Buster Keaton and Anita Page (especially the latter)

What UGA athlete won the 110-meter high hurdles, breaking the world record, at the Berlin Olympics in 1936?

Forrest "Spec" Towns

What other sport did he excel in, and what did he do after graduating?

Football, and he stayed on to coach the track team from 1938 to 1975 with time off for military service during World War II

"In football the object is to win. It doesn't matter who scores the points."

—**Charley Trippi**

Sports

"If you don't have passion, don't do it."
—Fran Tarkenton

What sport, instituted in 1928, lasted only as long as an R.O.T.C. cavalry unit was on campus through the 1930s?

Polo

What graduate of Notre Dame coached football from 1928 to 1937, compiling a 59-34-6 record, and really put UGA on the football map?

Harry Mehre

In November 1936 the football team visited the Polo Grounds in New York City and tied a powerful Fordham team with its "seven blocks of granite" (including Vince Lombardi) after coach Harry Mehre, a native of Indiana, stressed what in his pregame pep talk?

Revenge for defeat in the Civil War

Joel Hunt from Texas A & M was head football coach for only one year, 1938, but who was his line coach who took over and built a 22-year dynasty?

Wally Butts

> "He's [Uga] strictly a pet around here."
> —**Sonny Seiler**

In the 1930s women could earn a "G" by accumulating 1,000 points in what intramural athletics?

Riflery, swimming, basketball, tennis, dance, baseball, track, hiking, archery, horseback riding, and field hockey

When was the last time traditional rival Mercer played the Bulldogs in football and who won?

1941, and UGA won 81 to 0

Of the twenty-one contests between Mercer and UGA from 1892 to 1941, how many did UGA win?

All of them, with close calls in 1911 (8 to 5) and 1933 (13 to 12)

Which two world-class running backs played together on the powerful football team of 1942?

Frank Sinkwich and Charley Trippi

Who was the last football coach to recruit extensively in the North?

Wally Butts (1939 to 1960)

Who was the all-star guard, class of 1943, who was killed in action in Germany in November 1944 and whose widow received his silver star for gallantry at the homecoming game of 1945?

Walter "Chief" Ruark

Theron Sapp was an outstanding back, but what great achievement in 1957 secured his place as a football hero?

He scored UGA's only touchdown in a 7-0 victory over Georgia Tech that ended a terrible eight-game losing streak against the Jackets

Who was the tennis player, class of 1942, who returned to coach the team for thirty-four years, compiling a record of 706 wins 183 losses and making UGA a center for college tennis?

Dan Magill

> "I believe that challenges are the lifeblood of great teams and great athletes."
> —**Suzanne Yoculan**

Who was the able basketball coach who struggled along with mediocre talent in inadequate old Woodruff Hall from 1952 to 1965?

Harbin "Red" Lawson

What quarterback starred at Athens High School and UGA where he was both an athletic and academic All-American in 1960 and then shined for eighteen more years in the pros for the Giants and the Vikings?

Fran Tarkenton

Who was the first African American student to star in a major sport at UGA?

Ronnie Hogue in basketball from 1970 to 1973

Who were UGA's first African American football players in 1971?

Richard Appleby and Horace King (both from Athens) and Chuck Kinnebrew and Larry West

"Salesmanship is one of my best attributes."
—Jack Bauerle

What native of Gainsville was an All-American offensive lineman from 1974 to 1976 and starred with the Cincinnati Bengals from 1979 to 1985 and all along carried a distinctive nickname?

Mike "Moonpie" Wilson

What three football teams have claimed national titles?

1942 (one loss and recognized by some but not all polls as champ), 1946 (unbeaten but Notre Dame generally recognized as champ) and 1980 (unbeaten with final victory over Notre Dame in the Sugar Bowl for unanimous recognition as champ)

Who was the guest of honor at the Georgia-Kentucky homecoming game in 1977?

Prince Charles of Great Britain

> "But by far my greatest reward has been my association with countless other loyal Bulldogs, who are the very core of the university..."
> **—Dan Magill**

One of the great traditions at Sanford Stadium was the railroad embankment facing the east end zone where fanatic fans could cheer on their beloved Dawgs, but when was this ended by additional concrete stands?

At the end of the 1980 season

Who accompanied Herschel Walker and his human entourage to New York City in 1982 for the presentation of the Heisman Trophy?

Uga IV

Who was the professor who complained of special treatment for athletes, was fired, and eventually won an over a million dollar judgment in federal court in 1986?

Jan Kemp

In recent years what new area of sports has had spectacular success at UGA?

Women's athletics

Who were the two administrators who played crucial roles in this successful and rapid expansion?

Athletic Director Vince Dooley and Women's Athletic Director Liz Murphey

What coaches have spearheaded this dramatic success story?

Suzanne Yoculan (gymnastics), Andy Landers (basketball), and Jack Bauerle (swimming)

Who hosted UGA's national championship baseball team of 1990 at the White House?

President George Bush, formerly captain of Yale's baseball team

> "I've got a bulldog tattooed on my brain."
> —**Bill Goldberg**

Who was the recent basketball coach who compiled an impressive 45-19 record before moving on to Kentucky in 1998?

Tubby Smith

What is the famous slogan of UGA football teams, popular with Dawg fans (and also with opponents who question the school's academic standards)?

"How 'Bout Them Dawgs"

Of the thirteen UGA footballers in the College Hall of Fame, who are the four most recent inductees?

Bill Stanfield (1998), Herschel Walker (1999), Terry Hoage (2000), and Kevin Butler (2001)

> "UGA has one of the premier athletics programs in the nation."
>
> —Damon Evans

Who was UGA's greatest football coach?

Vince Dooley, who won a national championship in 1980 and compiled an overall record of 201 wins, 77 loses and 10 ties

What was a little unusual about his early coaching career?

After completing his eligibility as a quarterback, he earned an M.A. in history at Auburn while serving as an assistant coach

Who was a close second as top football coach, winning over 61% of his games from 1939 to 1960?

Wally Butts

Who was the most famous of UGA's real bulldog mascots, appearing in the movie *Midnight in the Garden of Good and Evil* and in April 1997 being proclaimed "Number One Mascot" by *Sports Illustrated*?

Uga V (deceased)

Who was his friend who also starred in the "Midnight" movie and now owns Uga VI?

Frank W. "Sonny" Seiler (B.B.A. 1956 and J.D. 1957)

What National Football Hall of Famer (1954) starred at UGA in the 1930s as a back and later served as a coach under Butts and Dooley?

Bill Hartman

What announcer, known as the "Voice of the Bulldogs," has covered football games on the radio since the late 1960s, and where is he from?

Larry Munson, a native of Minnesota, and he doesn't like grits

Who was his equally famous predecessor?

Ed Thilenius

Who was the greatest football player and all-round athlete in the school's history?

Debatable, of course, but one vote here for Charley Trippi (1942, 1945–1946)

Who was the school's greatest female athlete?

Teresa Edwards, All-American basketballer at UGA (1983–1986), pro star and five-time Olympic medalist

Who were UGA's two Heisman Trophy winners?

Frank Sinkwich in 1942 and Herschel Walker in 1982

What student from France, a rugby player, became an outstanding defensive lineman in 1987–1988?

Richard Tardits

> "We stepped on their face with a hobbed nailed boot and broke their nose."
> —**Larry Munson, referring to a 2001 victory over the Tennessee Volunteers**

What is the fiercest athletic rivalry in the Southeast?

Georgia-Georgia Tech, Alabama-Auburn and Florida against any neighbor are right up there, but Clemson-South Carolina tops them all—and helps illustrate why a disunited, quarrelsome South lost the Civil War

According to a recent, informal poll, who would Bulldog fans most like to defeat on the gridiron?

Auburn, Florida, and Georgia Tech (a three-way tie)

What solid but unspectacular running back who graduated in 1995 became a super-star in the pros?

Terrell Davis

"They talk about Southern hospitality, and I've never seen it more evident than at a Georgia game. It's as if you're invited into someone's home."

—**Chris Dufresne, national college football writer for the *Los Angeles Times***

What former UGA football star masterminded Atlanta's long-shot effort to gain the 1996 Olympics and then directed the whole complex operation?

Billy Payne (A.B. 1969 and J.D. 1973)

What Olympic events were hosted by UGA in 1996?

Volleyball, rhythmic gymnastics, and soccer

What is the most dramatic sports event in Sanford Stadium's long history?

The U.S. women's 2 to 1 soccer championship victory over China in the Olympic finals in 1996

Where did many of these young women play their college soccer?

The University of North Carolina

What significant renovation was required at Sanford Stadium to accommodate soccer?

Removal of the traditional hedges to broaden the field

Who trampled some of the new hedges following an upset win over Tennessee in 2000?

UGA fans

When did a UGA mascot personally intervene to ensure a football victory?

At Auburn in 1996, Georgia trailed as an Auburn runner scored a touchdown and hotdogged past Uga V; the Big Dawg lunged at the runner who was only saved from martyrdom by a strong handler with a strong leash; inspired, the other Dawgs rallied to prevail in overtime by a 56 to 49 count

What slogan relates directly to this dramatic incident?

"Let the Big Dawg Eat"

What UGA swimmer, three-time NCAA champion, won two gold medals at the Sydney Olympics in 2000?

Courtney Shealy

What UGA record was made and SEC record was tied in the 2001 football victory over Georgia Tech?

Billy Bennett kicked six consecutive field goals without a miss

What was the first band in the SEC to receive the Sudler Trophy, given annually to the most outstanding collegiate band?

The UGA Redcoat band, in October of 2000

> "If a skinny little girl from the small town of Cairo, Georgia, can travel the world bouncing a basketball in five Olympic Games, winning five Olympic medals, then so can you."
>
> —**Teresa Edwards, addressing UGA graduates**

Basketball coach Dennis Felton received what coaching honor in 2002?

Sun Belt Conference Coach of the Year

When football coach Mark Richt attended the University of Miami, he competed for the quarterback position with what emerging superstars?

Jim Kelly, Bernie Kosar, and Vinny Testaverde

What was the score of Georgia's victory over Florida State in the 2003 Sugar Bowl?

26-13

Further Reading

Who after World War II typed up a secret or at least unpublished, nineteen-volume *History of the University of Georgia,* which is available in the Hargrett Rare Book and Manuscript Library?

Registrar Thomas W. Reed

What is the best single-volume history of UGA covering only from 1785 to 1870?

E. Merton Coulter, *College Life in the Old South As Seen at the University of Georgia* (1928)

What are the two best single-volume histories of UGA?

Thomas G. Dyer, *The University of Georgia: A Bicentennial History, 1785–1985* (1985) and F.N. Boney, *A Pictorial History of the University of Georgia* (2000)

What is the best study of the growth of the physical plant at UGA?

Joel Thomas Bowen Jr., *Room to Grow: A Historical Analysis of the Physical Growth of the University of Georgia: 1785 to 1990* (dissertation, University of Georgia, 1990)

What is the best single-volume history of the desegregation of UGA?

Robert A. Pratt, *We Shall Not be Moved: The Desegregation of the University of Georgia* (2002)

What are three good books that cover the Athens area and thus add context to UGA's story?

Frances Taliaferro Thomas, *A Portrait of Historic Athens and Clarke County* (1992), Michael Thurmond, *A Story Untold: Black Men and Women in Athens History* (2001), and James K. Reap, *Athens: A Pictorial History* (2001)

So the long journey ends, but the story will continue for a long, long time. Stay tuned and remember: the best is yet to come!

ALSO OF INTEREST FROM HILL STREET PRESS

Damn Good Dogs!
The Real Story of Uga, the University of Georgia's Bulldog Mascots
Sonny Seiler & Kent Hannon

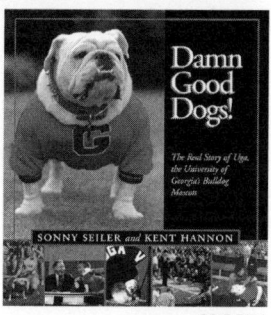

The definitive history of the beloved bulldogs named America's "No. 1 Mascot" by *Sports Illustrated*. Filled with hundreds of photos, illustrations, rare facts, and memorabilia.

SPORTS

> "Uga is inseparable from Georgia athletes. He's one of us!"
> —Vince Dooley

The Grit Cookbook
World-Wise, Down-Home Recipes
Ted Hafer & Jessica Greene

True to its Southern roots, the menu of Athens, Georgia, vegetarian eatery The Grit combines a soul-food sensibility with its meatless cuisine. Includes over 130 of The Grit's most requested recipes.

COOKBOOKS

> "The Grit has a far-flung reputation as the indie-rock Mosewood."
> —*The New Yorker*

Available wherever books are sold
Or call 1-800-925-0365   Visit **www.hillstreetpress.com**